The CHEROKEES
People of the Southeast

BY EILEEN LUCAS

NATIVE AMERICANS
THE MILLBROOK PRESS
BROOKFIELD, CONNECTICUT

Cover photo courtesy of Philbrook Museum of Art, Tulsa, Oklahoma
Photos courtesy of: Photo Researchers: pp. 8 (Bruce Roberts), 17
(Tomas Friedmann), 18 (Kenneth Murray), 52 (top, Lawrence Migdale;
bottom, Barbara Burnes); Frank H. McClung Museum, the University
of Tennessee at Knoxville: p. 13; Peabody Museum of Archaeology
and Ethnology, Harvard University: p. 15; National Museum of the
American Indian: p. 21 (clockwise from top left: #4593, #2183,
#3081); The Granger Collection: p. 24; Bettmann Archive: p. 27;
Smithsonian Institution: pp. 29, 46; Library of Congress: p. 32;
Woolaroc Museum, Bartlesville, Oklahoma: pp. 35, 41; Archives
& Manuscript Division of the Oklahoma Historical Society: pp. 36,
39, 44; Cherokee Nation of Oklahoma Communications: p. 49.

Library of Congress Cataloging-in-Publication Data
Lucas, Eileen.
The Cherokees : people of the Southwest / by Eileen Lucas.
p.   cm. — (Native Americans)
Includes bibliographical references (p.   ) and index.
Summary: Discusses the early history, beliefs, and daily life and
customs of the Cherokee Indians, their interaction with white
society, and the current status of the Cherokee Nation.
ISBN 1-56294-312-X (lib. bdg.)
1. Cherokee Indians—Juvenile literature. [1. Cherokee Indians.
2. Indians of North America.] I. Title. II. Series.
E99.C5L85 1993 973′.04975—dc20 92-40874 CIP AC

Published by The Millbrook Press
2 Old New Milford Road, Brookfield, CT 06804

CONTENTS

I wish to thank everyone who helped me
gather material for this book, especially
the people from Qualla Boundary,
Cherokee, North Carolina.

Special thanks to all my librarian friends,
particularly those at the Fontana library
in Wisconsin.

And a sincere thank-you to Cherokee crafts-
woman Pearl Wolf, who answered my questions
with patience and tolerance.

The Cherokees

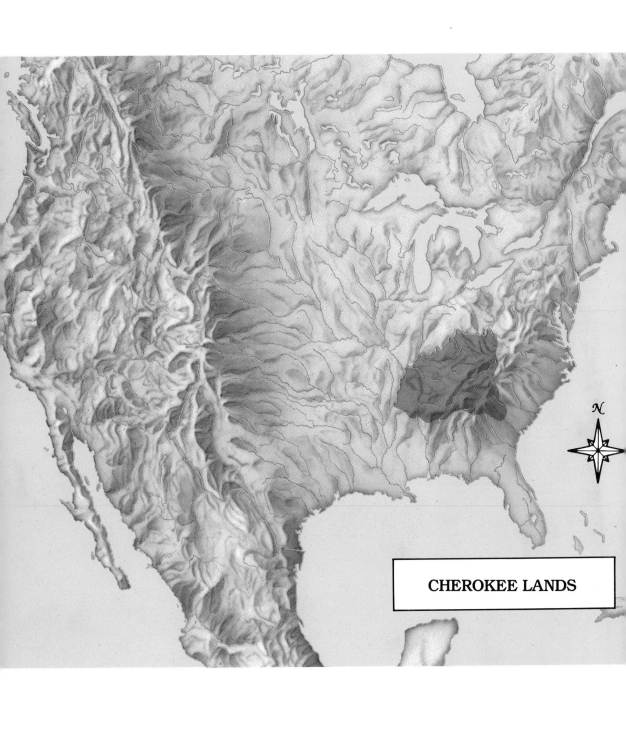

CHEROKEE LANDS

FACTS ABOUT
THE TRADITIONAL
CHEROKEE WAY OF LIFE

GROUP NAME:
Cherokee, or Ani Yun Wiya, the Principal People

CLANS:
Wolf, Paint, Bird, Deer, Long Hair, Blue, and Wild Potato

ORIGINAL HOMELAND:
Tennessee River valley and Great Smoky Mountain region

CURRENT POPULATION CENTERS:
Oklahoma (approximately 85,000 members)
North Carolina (approximately 9,000 members)

LANGUAGE:
Cherokee (Iroquoian family)

HOUSE TYPE:
Enclosed winter home of wattle and daub; open-air summer home

MAIN FOODS:
Mostly corn, also beans and squash; game, mostly deer and turkey

A modern Cherokee in ceremonial dress against the backdrop of the Great Smoky Mountains in North Carolina.

Chapter One

WHEN THIS WORLD WAS YOUNG

The Cherokees tell a story about how the world came to be. They say that long, long ago there were three worlds: Upper World, This World, and Lower World. In Upper World all was in order and harmony. In Lower World, however, all was in disorder, or chaos. This World, located between Upper World and Lower World, was a round island surrounded by water. Four cords attached This World to Upper World at points north, south, east, and west.

East was where the sun rose, so this was the direction of power and life. West was where the sun set, so this was the direction of darkness and death. North meant cold and trouble, while the South was warmth and peace.

A circle enclosing two perpendicular lines ⊕ became a symbol of This World and the four directions. It was a symbol of balance, because that was the purpose of This World, to provide balance between the perfect order of Upper World and the absolute chaos of Lower World.

Three kinds of creatures lived on This World in the beginning of time. There were winged creatures who could fly up toward Upper World. These were all the birds of the sky, including the mighty eagle and the lowly buzzard.

Then there were the creepy, crawly animals who lived closest to the disorderly Lower World. Among them were lizards, fish, and snakes, including the most fearsome of all—the rattler.

Four-legged creatures, such as the powerful bear and the swift-footed deer, walked on the surface of This World, providing balance between the two other groups.

Some creatures were seen as belonging to more than one group. For example, the frog had four feet, but lived close to the ground and swam like a fish.

One creature, Uktena, was the most evil of all creatures. This creature was a combination of snake, deer, and bird. To meet Uktena brought almost certain death. But the person who found one of its crystal scales, called *ulunsuti*, had a powerful charm that promised much luck.

THE PRINCIPAL PEOPLE ▪ Into this world of creatures came the people we call the Cherokees. They called themselves *Ani Yun Wiya*, the Principal People.

Anthropologists believe that people lived in the southeastern part of North America as far back as ten thousand years ago. The people who came to be known as Cherokees probably joined them about a thousand years ago.

The Cherokees were generally fairly tall and slim people. They wore clothes made from deerskin and painted their bodies with dyes made from roots and berries. They used sticks and a claylike mud to build their homes.

No one knows exactly where they came from or why, but evidence leads us to believe that they were a band of people related to the Iroquois Indians who lived to the north. They probably traveled along paths through the Appalachian Mountains until they came to the valley of the Tennessee River.

They believed that this land was given to them by the Great Spirit. Here they lived, worked, played, and died for many, many generations. Soon no one was alive who could remember a time when the Cherokees had lived anywhere else. And no one could imagine that the Cherokees would ever leave this land. It was their home.

MOUNTAIN HOMELAND ▪ The territory the Cherokee claimed for a homeland was more than 40,000 square miles (about 104,000 square kilometers) of forests, mountains, and river valleys. The Tennessee River and the Great Smoky Mountains were at the heart of this land. It was a beautiful and practical place to live. The fertile soil in the valleys, watered by creeks and rivers running down from the mountains, made excellent farmland. The forests on the mountainsides provided plentiful hunting grounds.

The Cherokees believed that mountains were home to spiritual creatures. The Little People were spirits who lived in caves. They could be friendly and helpful. But they could also make travelers lose their way. Anyone hunting in the mountains had to watch out for them.

Over the years, small changes and improvements were made in the way that they lived, but mostly the Principal People lived much as their ancestors had taught them, in harmony with the natural world. By making use of the things of nature they adapted to their environment and created a rich and satisfying culture.

Chapter Two

THE WAYS OF
THE ANCESTORS

To the north and west of the Great Smoky Mountains (in what is now Kentucky and Tennessee) were the Overhill Cherokee settlements. The Middle Cherokee villages lay to the east of the mountains (in what is now North Carolina), and the Lower Cherokee villages lay to the south (in what is now South Carolina and Georgia).

VILLAGES AND HOMES ▪ Cherokee villages generally had between thirty and fifty homes, but some of the most important ones had up to one hundred. A Cherokee home was usually built by bending and lashing sticks or poles together and then covering them with a claylike mud that hardened into a plaster. This mixture of sticks covered with mud was called wattle and daub. The roof was often covered with bark for extra protection from wind and rain. A hole in the roof let smoke escape from inside.

Inside the home was a cooking fire surrounded by mats and benches for sitting and lying, baskets for storing food and the rest of the family's belongings. These small round homes were

In the summer Cherokees lived in open rectangular houses (right), while in the winter they moved to smaller, warmer homes called asi *(left).*

called *asi.* They provided protection when the weather was bad and were used mostly during the winter months. During the warm summer months, families spent most of their time outside and lived in open-walled structures with bark- and grass-covered roofs.

During warm weather Cherokees wore few clothes, and young children generally wore nothing at all. At other times of the year Cherokees wore shirts, skirts, cloaks, and moccasins made from deerskin.

At the center of each village was an open area, or square, and a town house. The square was where village ceremonies, dances, and games were held. Covered platforms often lined the square. Villagers sat in these during warm weather to watch activities in the square.

The town house was the place where community decisions were made. It was generally a circular or six-sided structure, large enough for all the people of the village to sit inside. Benches lined the walls, and a low fire burned in the center. This was the sacred fire, which played an important part in many ceremonies.

CLAN AND KINSHIP ▪ There were seven Cherokee clans: the Wolf, Paint, Bird, Deer, Long Hair, Blue, and Wild Potato. (The names of the last three clans are sometimes translated in different ways.) A man and a woman had to be from different clans in order to marry.

In Cherokee society, people were related only through their mother's side of the family. When a Cherokee couple married, they moved into the woman's house. Sometimes the man lived with his wife and children, sometimes not. Either way, it was the wife's brothers (the children's uncles) who taught the young boys to hunt and to develop other needed skills. If a man left his wife and children, he moved in with his sister and her children, and it was his responsibility to teach them what they needed to know.

Stickball

Cherokees played many games, but stickball was one of the most popular. Before a game there was feasting, dancing, and singing. Players painted their bodies as if for war. Sometimes called "the little brother of war," stickball often became extremely violent. In fact, sometimes disputes between Cherokees and other groups of Indians were settled by a stickball match.

Each player held two sticks, each about 2 to 3 feet (.6 to .9 meters) long. At the end of each stick was a loop of hide with animal sinew or skin strung across it, forming a sort of cup to hold the ball. The ball was a small piece of softened deer hide stuffed with hair and sewn together.

The players for each team gathered at opposite ends of the field. A team might have as many as one hundred players. The ball was thrown into the air, and the game was on.

The object of the game was to get the ball through the goalposts at the other end of the field. Just about any behavior on the field was allowed. It was not unusual for players to be severely hurt or even killed during these contests. There was a great deal of screaming and yelling on and off the field, especially when points were scored. The game was over when one team scored a certain number of points, usually twelve.

LEADERSHIP ▪ Cherokees almost never put one person in charge of an entire village. Since each village was made up of several clans, there might be a leader for each one. A distinguished warrior might serve as leader for matters relating to war, and there might be another person in charge of matters relating to the village itself and to peace.

Both men and women could be leaders. A particularly respected female leader was often called a Beloved Woman, just as a highly respected male leader might be called a Beloved Man.

Villagers listened to anyone who had something to say on a particular subject, and everyone joined in making decisions affecting the whole community. The Cherokees were in fact a very democratic group.

COMMUNITY LIFE ▪ Children were expected to behave according to the teachings of the elders. Cherokees did not believe in spanking their children. Instead, children who misbehaved were told stories about bad things that happened to naughty children. If they did not want to be eaten by bears or captured by evil spirits as the bad children in the stories were, they would learn to behave.

Children were also expected to help out however they could. They might be set to work gathering firewood or picking berries. Older children might be in charge of watching out for younger ones. And there was plenty of time for play, too. But even when at play, Cherokee children were usually learning skills that would be helpful to them as they grew up.

In a Cherokee village, men, women, and children joined in taking care of the community. There were jobs enough for all.

A Cherokee woman grinds corn into meal with a mortar and pestle in the old way.

Men cleared the fields, and women planted and tended the crops. Cherokees raised corn, beans, squash, and a few other vegetables. Many of these crops were planted in between rows of corn to conserve space.

Corn was the primary crop and main staple of the Cherokee diet. Some was eaten fresh, much as we eat corn today. Some was dried and stored for the winter. Then it was ground into a flour that could be mixed with water and baked or fried. Sometimes corn flour was wrapped in corn husks and boiled.

Besides farming, women gathered edible berries and roots. They also added variety to the diet by preserving and preparing food in different ways. Men were usually responsible for hunting. In order to be good hunters, boys had to learn not only to use weapons, but also to move silently through the forest and to imitate animal sounds. All these skills were necessary if Cherokees were to eat well.

A girl shows how to shoot darts through a blow gun. Cherokees still use this ancient weapon to hunt game today.

Cherokees used the animals they killed in many ways. Besides meat, turkeys provided feathers for many ceremonial uses. Bears were prized for their warm fur, their claws, and their fat, as well as for their meat. And, of course, nearly every part of a slain deer was used in some way. The skins were scraped, then soaked and dried and stretched and sewn into garments. From muscle sinew came thread, and needles were made from chips of bone.

CEREMONIES AND BELIEFS ▪ Cherokees were respectful of the natural world. A Cherokee hunter always apologized to the spirit of an animal he killed. He explained that his family needed food and clothing, and he thanked the animal for giving its life.

This respect for the creations of the Great Spirit was at the heart of all that Cherokees believed in. It was part of their religion and their way of life. What Cherokees believed and how they lived were tied to the concept that all of nature was related.

Because corn played an important role in Cherokee life, there were many ceremonies involved in the planting and growing of corn. A special ceremony was performed when the dried kernels saved from the previous year were planted. Another ceremony marked the beginning of the harvest. The third and largest ceremony took place at the "full ripening" of the crop in the early fall.

This ceremony was called the Busk, or Green Corn Ceremony. The celebration of the Busk marked the end of the old year and the beginning of the new. In honor of this occasion all the homes in the village and the town house were cleaned and given fresh mats. All the cooking fires and even the sacred fire in the town house were put out. Then there would be a day of fasting, followed by a day of feasting. On this day all crimes of the past year (except murder) were forgiven. A new fire was set in the town house by the village *Adawehis*, or holy man. The women took coals from this ceremonial fire to light fresh fires in their own homes. The feasting was followed by a ritual bath to purify everyone for the new year.

CHEROKEE CRAFTS ▪ Many of the things that we consider "crafts" were very important items in everyday Cherokee life. Others were saved for special occasions and ceremonies. Baskets held the roots and berries gathered from the countryside as well as the vegetables grown in the fields. Clay pots held water and cooked foods. Sculptors carved tools, weapons, and pipes.

The materials for these objects were abundant in the Cherokees' homeland. Clay for pots was dug from the ground and baked in a fire. Sticks and stones were often used to scrape designs in the clay. Grasses, vines, and other plant fibers, including corn husks, were the raw materials for baskets. The juices of nuts, roots, and berries were used to dye these fibers and add color to the baskets. Cherokee crafters wanted their creations to be attractive as well as useful. It was said that baskets were the Indian woman's poems. Cherokee pipes, very important in many ceremonies, were beautifully carved.

Also important in many ceremonies were a variety of masks and rattles. Some masks looked like the heads of animals. Others were made to look like scary faces. They were usually carved from buckeye and other kinds of wood. Cherokees used these masks, which they called booger masks, to make fun of their enemies.

A splint basket and a clay jar carved
with a woven design show the artistry of
the Cherokees. Booger masks were carved
from wood and painted with natural dyes.
A strip of fur served as hair.

Rattles and Noisemakers

Cherokees have used rattles and noisemakers in their cere-monies since ancient times. They made these instruments from things they found in the world around them.

A walk through the woods or along a stream can pro-vide items you can use to make your own instruments. Be on the lookout for any of the following: pebbles, shells, sticks, berries, nuts, feathers, and bones. In your kitchen, you can probably find foods that were also stored in Cher-okee homes: dried beans and dried corn (popcorn).

Cherokees used gourds, small pumpkins, and squashes for rattles; or they made them out of baskets or molded clay.

You can turn a gourd into a rattle by putting it away in a dark, dry place, such as a closet, for several months. The pulp will dry out, and the seeds will be left to "rattle around."

You can change the sound of the rattle by poking a hole in the gourd with a sharp knife. Then, when the inside of the gourd has dried up, you can fill the cavity with pebbles or dried beans or corn. After filling the gourd, plug the hole with a stick.

Cherokees made paints from berries, leaves, roots, and nuts. You might want to use your own mixed paints in-stead. You can decorate your gourd like the Cherokees did by tying feathers, nuts, or tiny sticks to it with string.

Even if you don't have a gourd to turn into a rattle, you can make a noisemaker by tying bones, small sticks, and nuts to pieces of string and then shaking them together.

When these masks were worn in ceremonies, dancers usually wore or carried rattles as well. Rattles were used to make noise either to get the attention of a good spirit or to scare away evil. Rattles could be simply several bones strung together or intricately decorated hides stuffed with seeds or stones. Cherokees sometimes used turtle shells filled with corn kernels as rattles. Cherokee women were known to tie five of these rattles on each leg under their skirts for special dances.

WARFARE AND RELATIONS WITH NEIGHBORS ▪ The main reason to go to war was to seek revenge for a previous attack by an enemy. Thus warfare was generally seen as the means of keeping things in balance. Among the Cherokees and their enemies, preparing for or defending against such attacks was serious business. From childhood, boys were trained in the use of such weapons as darts, slings, clubs, and bow and arrows. While these weapons were used mainly for hunting, they also served as instruments of war.

A war party was usually made up of about twenty to thirty men. Occasionally women went, too. Members of the war party performed special ceremonies. Before leaving the safety of their village, they fasted and prayed. They painted their bodies with dyes made from roots and berries. They often purified themselves by drinking a special "black drink," which made them vomit. After leaving their village, they traveled quietly, often in single file, in hopes of surprising their enemy. After the attack, the Cherokee party returned home. The war was over, until, of course, the enemy came looking for revenge.

*Tahchee, a Cherokee war chief also served
as a guide for the United States Army.*

The Cherokees battled most frequently with the Creeks. The Creeks were a large and powerful people whose territory lay mostly to the south of the Cherokees. Sometimes the two groups fought for control of hunting grounds. Usually they fought for revenge after an attack by the other. Whatever the reason, battles were usually fought between small war parties rather than between whole tribes.

Another neighboring tribe was the Chickasaw. Sometimes the Cherokees and their Chickasaw neighbors were allies, and sometimes they were enemies. When the Shawnees tried to move into Cherokee and Chickasaw territory from the west, these two groups united to fight them. After a number of battles, the Shawnees were finally driven out of the area.

The Cherokees were aware that these different groups of people were like them in some ways and very different in others. One of the things that set the Cherokees apart from their neighbors was their language. Cherokees spoke an Iroquoian language related to that of Iroquois to the north. Many of the tribes in southeastern North America spoke other languages called Muskogean. In fact, that's probably where the name Cherokee comes from. Neighboring tribes called the Cherokees *Tsalagi*, which means people of a different speech.

These then were the things that defined the Cherokees as a group of people—their clan and kinship system, their language, and their belief in the teachings of their elders, especially their belief in the importance of keeping things in balance. This was the purpose in almost everything they did.

THE CHEROKEE
STORY

For many generations Cherokees continued to live according to the ways of their ancestors. From time to time a new crop was introduced or a new tool was developed, but life was basically good, and the teachings of the old ones made sense.

STRANGERS IN THE LAND ▪ In 1540 the Spaniard Hernando de Soto passed through a portion of Cherokee territory. He was probably the first white man the Cherokees ever saw. He was looking for gold to take back to Spain. Not finding any in Cherokee territory, he moved on. He enslaved and killed many Indians in the Southeast, but he had little noticeable effect on the Cherokees. They had no way of knowing that this small party of white men would be followed by hundreds and thousands more.

And they had no way of knowing that the strange and deadly new diseases that began to spread through their villages had been brought by foreigners. Almost immediately after the arrival of the Spanish, and off and on over the following centuries, epidemics of smallpox, measles, and cholera wiped out whole

A drawing of "Discovery of the Mississippi by De Soto A.D. 1541," by William H. Powell.

villages and large portions of Native American tribes. The fact that Indian healers could do little to prevent or cure these diseases was one of the first threats to traditional Indian beliefs.

Occasionally there was word of strangely dressed travelers in their territory. At first it was the Spanish, looking for gold and slaves. Later it was an occasional Frenchman, coming up from the Mississippi River valley, usually looking to trade guns and household items for animal skins. Later still there were English visitors who also were interested in animal skins. The Cherokees found that they could get useful things from these men, such as sewing needles and cooking pots made from metal. As long as these newcomers behaved, Cherokees generally accepted their presence.

SETTLERS AND SOLDIERS ■ By the early 1700s explorers and traders were followed by missionaries and settlers, people who planned to stay. And the three European nations were fighting with one another over who would control the land of the so-called New World. As they argued over who owned this territory, they gave little thought to the fact that it was already claimed by the Indians. Since they did not see fancy houses, big cities, and fenced-in farms, they considered the land vacant and available. By the mid-1700s there were European settlements scattered throughout Cherokee territory.

Marriages between white men and Indian women became common. This further weakened the traditional Cherokee way of life as the children of these marriages often adopted European ways. These children were still Cherokees because their mothers were Cherokees. But they were being raised differently than traditional Cherokee children.

These seven Cherokee chiefs (Attakullaculla is at the far right) travelled to London, where they spoke with King George II.

Most of the settlers in Cherokee country were from England. The British government wanted the Cherokees to help them defeat their Spanish and French enemies in North America. In 1730 seven Cherokee leaders were taken to London to visit King George II. This pleased the Cherokees and strengthened their tie with the British. They were even more pleased when the British government promised to keep new settlers out of their territory.

One of the Cherokee leaders was Attakullaculla, also known as Little Carpenter. Attakullaculla was a great diplomat. He worked very hard to keep peace between the Cherokees and the British. When a terrible smallpox epidemic killed nearly half the Cherokee population in 1738, some of the Cherokees blamed the British. They wanted to join the French to attack the British colonists. But Attakullaculla convinced them not to.

Meanwhile the British colonists paid no attention to the promise that their king had made to the Cherokees. They felt they had the right to settle wherever they wanted, even in Cherokee land.

Still the Cherokees hoped to keep things in balance. They learned from the settlers. Some Cherokees built homes of logs like those of the white settlers. Cherokee women bought ready-made cloth for clothes, which was much easier to work with than hides. In fact, most deerskins were now given to traders and shipped to Europe. Hunting was no longer just for food and clothing. It was business.

The Cherokees were willing to teach things of value to the white settlers as well. They hoped that by sharing what they had with the settlers they could live together on the land.

But the settlers did not want to share the land. They wanted to own it. No matter how much the Cherokees gave up, the settlers would never be satisfied until they had it all.

BRITISH ALLIES ▪ The Cherokees took the side of the British in the French and Indian War. This was partly because of their friendship with the English king, and partly because several of their traditional Indian enemies were fighting with the French.

Nanye hi, a Beloved Woman

One of the greatest Cherokee leaders was Nanye hi, a member of the Wolf Clan and a niece of Attakullaculla.

When her husband, a Cherokee warrior named Kingfisher, joined a war party to fight the Creeks in 1754, Nanye hi, a mother of two, went with him. The battle was fierce, and the Cherokees were losing, when Kingfisher was killed. Nanye hi took up his weapons and fought in his place. This rallied the rest of the Cherokees, and they won the battle.

Word spread of the young woman's courage. She was honored by her people with the title *Ghigau*, which means Beloved Woman. She worked closely with her uncle, Attakullaculla, urging her people to live in peace and not to give up any more of their land.

In 1757 she married an English trader named Bryant Ward and became known among the white people as Nancy Ward. Soon afterward, she had another child, a daughter named Elizabeth.

Besides her own children and later her grandchildren, Nanye hi took care of many Cherokee orphans. And she continued to work for peace between the Cherokees and the settlers. At the signing of a peace treaty in 1781 she said "this peace must last forever." But the fighting went on.

Nancy Ward, the Beloved Woman Nanye hi, died in 1817. Sadly, in 1838 most of her people were forced to leave their homeland, but wherever Cherokees live today, the memory of Nanye hi lives, too.

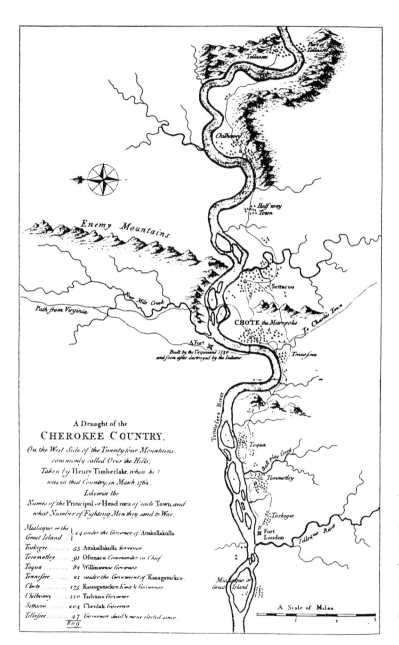

A Draught of the
CHEROKEE COUNTRY,
On the West Side of the Twenty four Mountains,
commonly called Over the Hills;
Taken by Henry Timberlake, when he
was in that Country, in March 1762.
Likewise the
Names of the Principal or Head men of each Town, and
what Number of Fighting Men they send to War.

Mialaquo, or the   } 24 under the Governor of Attakullakulla.
Great Island.
Toskegee.........55 Attakullakulla Governor.
Tommotley......91 Ostenaco Commander in Chief.
Toqua.........84 Willinawaw Governor.
Tennessee......21 under the Government of Kanagatucko.
Chote........175 Kanagatucko King & Governor.
Chilhowey.....110 Yachtino Governor.
Settacoo.....204 Cheulah Governor.
Tellassee......47 Governor dead & none elected since.
                 809

Listed on
this 1765 map,
drawn during
the French and
Indian War, are
the numbers of
warriors Atta-
kullaculla sent
into battle.

■ 32 ■

Throughout the war, Cherokee territory was the scene of frequent battles. Colonists attacked Indian villages; Indian war parties attacked settlements and enemy Indian villages; British soldiers and their Indian allies attacked French soldiers and their Indian allies. Both sides did terrible things.

Eventually the British defeated the French, but that did not really bring peace. Fighting continued between Cherokees and colonists, and more colonists were invading Cherokee territory all the time.

In 1775 the colonists went to war with Britain. Because of their friendship with the British king, the Cherokees sided with the British.

When the Americans won their Revolution, the Cherokees were on the losing side. They were forced to give up most of their territory to the American government. In return they were promised that the rest of their land would remain theirs forever.

But in the 1790s and early 1800s many more treaties were signed. Each time the American government took a little more of the Cherokee homeland. Each time the Cherokees were promised that the rest would remain theirs forever.

Some of the Cherokees got tired of dealing with white people and seeing their land taken away. They moved farther west to land that was still wilderness in what is now Arkansas.

TO PROTECT THE LAND ▪ Many Cherokees who stayed behind continued to adapt to the new ways of life. Their main objective was to protect their remaining lands. They hoped to do this by showing the Americans that they would be "good neighbors." They raised sheep, goats, hogs, and cattle. They added cotton, grains, and indigo (a plant used to make blue dye) to their fields. They were especially skilled at spinning cloth, weaving baskets, and making jewelry. Missionaries were allowed to set up schools where Cherokee children learned to read and write English.

Until 1821 there was no written Cherokee language, only a spoken one. A Cherokee named Sequoyah had given a lot of thought to this. He'd seen that a written language gave the British and Americans power to communicate over great distances. He wanted the Cherokees to have that power, too. By assigning a symbol to each sound in the Cherokee language he created a kind of alphabet called a syllabary. When he was done he taught it to many of the Cherokee people. Soon most of them could read and write in their own language.

The creation of the Cherokee syllabary is a good example of how the Cherokees kept important aspects of their own culture even as they adapted to some of the settlers' ways. Another example of this was the writing of the Cherokee constitution in 1827. This document was modeled after the United States Constitution, but its purpose was to protect the Cherokee people. It formally established a Cherokee Nation in hopes of keeping the Cherokee homeland.

The Cherokee Nation began publishing a newspaper called the *Cherokee Phoenix* in 1828. Edited by a well-educated, mixed-blood Cherokee named Elias Boudinot and written in both Cherokee and English, it was read by many Americans as well as Cherokees.

Also in 1828, John Ross, another mixed-blood Cherokee, was elected principal chief of the Cherokees. He had a full-blood Cherokee wife named Quatie, and was well liked by both the

In 1821 Sequoyah invented a system of writing
called a syllabary, in which each character stood
for a syllable in the Cherokee language.

John Ross, principal chief of the Cherokees.

mixed-blood and full-blood members of the Cherokee community. His Indian name was Cooweescoowee. He would serve as principal chief until 1839, then chief of the united Cherokee Nation until his death in 1866. The last forty years of his life were the most difficult times the Cherokee people had ever known.

REMOVAL ■ In 1828 a new American president was elected as well. His name was Andrew Jackson. He was considered a hero of frontier wars. He seemed to forget that on many occasions the Cherokees had been his allies and had fought bravely by his side. He was determined to see that all Indians were removed from the southeastern United States. He was supported in this by many government officials, especially in Georgia, where leaders demanded that Jackson remove all Indians from "their" land.

Georgia claimed that the Cherokee Nation was merely a county in the state of Georgia. When gold was discovered in Cherokee territory, a law was passed making it illegal for Cherokees to mine gold on their own land. It was also illegal for Cherokees to testify in court against white persons. It was becoming more and more difficult for the Cherokees to survive.

In 1830 the Indian Removal Act was passed, giving President Jackson the authority to remove all Indians from the southeastern United States. This applied to the Cherokees and their neighbors the Creeks, Chickasaws, Choctaws, and Seminoles. Together these groups were known as the Five Civilized Tribes because of their well-developed cultures and the achievements of their peoples. But civilized or not, they were told they had to leave their sacred homelands.

The Cherokee people were torn about how to react. An old Cherokee leader named Whitepath suggested that the Cherokee abandon all the white man's ways and go back to their traditional way of living. Some of the younger leaders wanted to accept the white man's order and move west. John Ross called for a moderate path. He knew that the Cherokees could not turn back the hands of time. There would be no returning to the old ways. But he still hoped that by being good neighbors, perhaps the Cherokees could continue to live in their ancestral homeland in peace.

The United States Supreme Court tried to defend the Cherokees' rights, but President Jackson ignored its rulings. In 1833 the government of Georgia held a lottery, granting ownership of Cherokee land to white people. Even the beautiful home of John Ross was claimed by Georgians. Ross was forced to move his family to Tennessee.

THE TREATY OF NEW ECHOTA ▪ Some of the Cherokees decided that the time had come to move west. They feared that soon everything belonging to them would be gone. Their leader was named Major Ridge. While Ridge and his group of Cherokees prepared to head west, John Ross went to Washington, D.C., to try to negotiate with the U.S. government.

In December 1835, while Ross was gone, Major Ridge and a small group of Cherokees signed a treaty with United States agents. This became known as the Treaty of New Echota. They gave the government what it had been asking for—*all* Cherokee land in the East. In return the Cherokees would receive land in Indian Territory, in what is now Oklahoma, and five million dollars to pay the cost of moving.

Major Ridge was supported by only a few of the approximately sixteen thousand Cherokee people. The rest of the Cherokee Nation were furious with him for signing the treaty and giving up their land. They claimed that this treaty was not binding because the majority of the Cherokee people had not agreed to it. But the U.S. Congress ratified the treaty and it became law. General Winfield Scott was given orders to round up all the Cherokees and see to their removal.

Meanwhile, members of Major Ridge's "Treaty Party" began moving west, joining the so-called "Old Settlers" who had moved there a decade or two earlier. But the rest of the Cherokees tried to ignore the treaty. John Ross referred to it as "that dirty paper," and continued to fight against it in Washington. The people went on planting their crops.

Then suddenly in the summer of 1838, soldiers appeared and ordered the Cherokees to come with them. Families were dragged from their homes and fields with nothing but the clothes

*Major Ridge signed the Treaty of New Echota
in which he agreed that the Cherokees would give
up their homeland and move to Oklahoma.*

on their backs. Children were separated from their parents. No sooner were Cherokee homes emptied than white settlers moved in, claiming their land and their belongings.

THE TRAIL OF TEARS ▪ Stockades were built in North Carolina, Georgia, Tennessee, and Alabama to house the Cherokees until their journey could begin. The summer was stiflingly hot in the stockades. In June the first group began the journey. They were herded onto boats and sent down the Tennessee River. Two more groups followed soon after. The boats were crowded. There wasn't much food, and much of what there was was rotten. Many people got sick from the heat and the terrible conditions.

The rest of the people were allowed to wait until fall to start the journey. They hoped that the weather would be better. They also decided to travel overland instead of by river. Wagons and horses were hired for the sick and elderly, but many people would make the entire 1,000-mile (1,600-kilometer) journey on foot. Some groups made the journey in just over one hundred days. For others it took nearly twice that long.

The winter turned out to be unusually cold. The people were short of clothing and blankets. Many died of the cold. John Ross's wife, Quatie, died of pneumonia after giving up her blanket to a sick child. Each night the weary travelers would bury the people who had died that day. They called the journey *Nuna da ut sun y,* the place where they cried. We have come to know it as the Trail of Tears. In 1988 it was named a National Historic Trail in recognition of the misery that was inflicted there. Of the twelve to fourteen thousand people who were forced to make the journey, about four thousand died along the way.

*A third of the Cherokee people died on the
tragic journey called the Trail of Tears.*

TSALI'S STAND ▪ It took a long time for all the Cherokee people to be rounded up and removed. During this time, a few managed to evade the soldiers by hiding in the dense forests and rocky caves of the Great Smoky Mountains. While four thousand of their people were dying along the Trail of Tears, these Indians fought to stay alive, living on roots and nuts and what small game they could catch.

One of these was a Cherokee farmer named Tsali. In October of 1838 he and his family were being taken by soldiers to a stockade to join the others being sent west. One of the soldiers mistreated Tsali's wife. A scuffle broke out. A soldier was killed. Tsali and his family fled into the Great Smoky Mountains and hid in a cave that awful winter.

Finally word came to Tsali that if he and his party would give themselves up, the rest of the Cherokees hiding in the mountains would be left alone. So Tsali, his brother, and his oldest son turned themselves in. They were shot in punishment for the death of the soldier. In later years, the story of Tsali's bravery and love for his homeland would be told and retold by the descendants of the Cherokees who hid out in those mountains.

Those Cherokees who escaped the soldiers joined another group of Cherokees who had been living along the Oconaluftee River in North Carolina. Most of these people still followed the traditional ways of the Cherokees. Together, these people and their descendants became known as the Eastern Band of the Cherokees. A white man who grew up among them, W. H. Thomas, helped purchase land for them in the foothills of the Smokies. This became known as the Qualla Boundary Cherokee Reservation.

STARTING OVER ▪ Meanwhile the Western Band of the Cherokees was trying to start a new life in Indian Territory. There were many problems. Food and other provisions were in very short supply. And there were now several very different groups of Cherokees, each with their own idea of how things should be run.

First there were the Old Settlers who had moved west earlier in the 1800s. Then there were the members of the Treaty Party who had moved west with Major Ridge. And finally there were the most recent and most numerous immigrants, the National Party supporters of John Ross. The differences between these groups made it difficult for the Cherokee people to live as one nation in the West. Between 1838 and 1846 these groups tottered on the brink of civil war.

Despite their conflicts, the Cherokee people slowly rebuilt their world. In 1839 they established a new capital in Tahlequah, with a sturdy brick capitol building at its center. They wrote a new constitution and reelected John Ross as principal chief. In 1846 they signed a treaty among themselves, pledging to live as one people once again. The Cherokees were working hard to rise again to the standard of living they had enjoyed in their homeland in the 1820s.

When the American Civil War broke out, the Cherokees tried to remain neutral. They had enough problems without this white man's war. But again the Cherokee people were torn. Chief John Ross believed that the Cherokee people owed their allegiance to the federal government of the United States. But the Cherokees had come from the South. Many of their farming practices were much like those of southern planters. Some Cherokee farmers even owned slaves.

The Confederate government put a great deal of pressure on the Cherokee Nation to join the Confederacy. A Cherokee named Stand Watie led a group of Cherokees to fight for the Confederacy. Some Cherokees fought on the Union side, too. Numerous battles and much guerrilla fighting took place on Cherokee land during the Civil War. Many houses were burned and farms destroyed. Many Cherokee children were made orphans.

Cherokee leader Stand Watie was a Confederate general during the Civil War.

The Civil War was a terrible disaster for the Cherokee Nation. After the war more Cherokee land was taken away. The Cherokees found themselves once again in the process of rebuilding their homes and businesses. With very little money and few friends in the U.S. government, the Cherokees were facing grim times.

Also after the war, more white people began moving west. Railroad tracks were laid through Indian Territory. In 1904 oil was discovered there. Once again white settlers wanted the land that had been given to the Indians. Many of these settlers considered all Indians "savages," even though most of the Indians were better educated than the white settlers entering the Territory.

Several Indian groups suggested that Indian Territory should become a state in the United States. It would be called Sequoyah. Instead, Indian Territory and Oklahoma Territory were joined into one state, Oklahoma, in 1907. As citizens of Oklahoma, the Cherokees struggled throughout the early part of the twentieth century to try to balance their needs as the Principal People with the demands of the modern world.

THE EASTERN BAND ▪ Meanwhile, times were tough for the Eastern Cherokees, too. Some of them participated in the Civil War as members of the Legion of Confederates led by their old friend W. H. Thomas. After being captured by Union soldiers, some Cherokee members of Thomas's legion joined the Union Army instead.

In 1868 the Eastern Band was officially recognized as separate from the Western Band. Work groups called *gadugi* were formed to protect Cherokee workers and their way of life. Members of a *gadugi* helped each other when they were sick and

*A cabin on the Qualla Reservation
in North Carolina, 1888.*

pooled their resources for the benefit of all. In 1889 the Eastern Band officially became a corporation to protect the property and businesses of the community.

A Cherokee medicine man named Swimmer shared a great deal of information about traditional Cherokee ways with anthropologist James Mooney during the 1890s. Swimmer told of Kana ti and Selu, the first man and woman of Cherokee legend. Many traditional ways that might otherwise have been lost when Swimmer died in 1899 were thus recorded.

During the early 1900s there was a boom in the timber industry in the Great Smoky Mountain area occupied by the Eastern Cherokees. This provided jobs for some Cherokees, although more often than not the Cherokees found themselves discriminated against and paid less than white workers doing the same jobs.

When most of the best trees for wood were gone, so were many of the best jobs that had been open to Cherokees. During the Great Depression, when so many people in the United States suffered for lack of jobs, conditions were very bad on the Cherokee Reservation. Government-sponsored programs helped a little, but the biggest help was the creation of the Great Smoky Mountain National Park. Many visitors would come to see the beautiful mountains, and in so doing, they would help provide jobs for the people who lived there.

Chapter Four

CHEROKEES TODAY

The struggle for balance that has always been part of the Cherokee way of life continues.

During the World Wars, young Cherokee men joined the United States armed services. After World War II some of these veterans and other young Cherokees left their communities to seek educational and business opportunities in other parts of the country. Today people of Cherokee heritage can be found making a living in just about all careers in many places. It is estimated that there are more than 100,000 people of at least partial Cherokee descent living in the United States.

For some, being Cherokee means simply having ancestors of Cherokee blood. For others, it is a matter of culture as well as ancestry. These people have remained in touch with what it traditionally means to be Cherokee.

The majority of people who still call themselves Cherokee live in Oklahoma or North Carolina.

OKLAHOMA ▪ There are about 85,000 members of the Cherokee Nation in Oklahoma today. Wilma Mankiller was elected principal

*Wilma Mankiller, principal chief of
the Cherokee Nation in Oklahoma.*

chief in 1985. Born among poor Cherokees in eastern Oklahoma, Mankiller is personally aware of the problems that many of her people face. She is the first woman elected principal chief, but she follows in the footsteps of other great female Cherokee leaders. She is dedicated to leading Cherokees and all Native American tribes to a better way of life.

The Cherokee Nation in Oklahoma is a complex political, economic, and social organization. It operates a replica of a Cherokee village of the 1700s, a museum, and a library. In an outdoor theater the play *Trail of Tears* is performed by a largely Indian cast. In these places Cherokees and other Americans can come to learn and to appreciate the history and culture of the Principal People.

In 1986 a business called Cherokee Gardens was established. This creative enterprise provides jobs for Cherokees and income for the Nation. Other businesses operated by the Nation include.a ranch and a lodge with banquet facilities. Leaders of the Cherokees plan to continue these efforts to bring funds into the Nation so that the people's lives can be bettered.

QUALLA BOUNDARY ▪ The Eastern Band in North Carolina has about 9,000 members. Jonathan Taylor has been their principal chief since 1987. He has many years of service in tribal government to his credit. He states that his main objective is "jobs, jobs, and jobs."

Since the opening of the Great Smoky Mountains National Park, in 1934, the Eastern Cherokees have taken advantage of the large number of tourists that travel through their land. Cherokee, North Carolina, the heart of the Qualla Boundary, is also one of the main entrances to the park. Visitors stopping in Cherokee can view many aspects of Cherokee life, past and present. The play *Unto These Hills,* a dramatic presentation of Cherokee history, is performed each summer. The Oconaluftee Indian Village is an authentic replica of a Cherokee village of the mid-1700s. The Museum of the Cherokee Indian contains a great deal of information about the Cherokee people from the very beginnings of their history through the present time.

But Cherokee, North Carolina, is not just a place to learn about the past. As part of the Qualla Boundary, it is very much part of the present. It is where children go to school, and adults work to earn a living. Community action groups were formed during hard times in the 1930s and 1940s. These groups developed programs to improve living conditions for poorer members of the community. These groups continue to work today to raise the living standards of the Cherokee community.

Probably one of the most important business decisions of the Eastern Band was the creation of the Qualla Arts and Crafts Mutual in 1947. This organization markets the crafts of nearly two hundred Cherokee men and women. A Farmers Co-op was also formed to sell the produce of Cherokee farmers. By working together and pooling their resources, the Cherokee people are able to operate more efficiently for the greater benefit of their community.

ALWAYS A NEW BEGINNING ▪ Like other Native Americans, Cherokees live together on reservation land and as individuals in general society. Some have accepted most, if not all, of the ways of modern American society. Others wish to remain as close to the

For members of the Cherokee Nation today, ancient traditions are remembered, but life goes on as usual, too.

ancient ways as possible. Many travel a road somewhere in between. They share with other Native Americans the struggle to keep their unique identity as Indians while trying to live successfully in America. Their legal status is generally very complicated. It reflects both their right to self-reliance as well as to special benefits the government gives to tribal members.

In recent years efforts have been made to increase contact between the Cherokees in North Carolina and those in Oklahoma. In April 1984, there was a reunion of Eastern and Western Cherokee councils at the Red Clay Historical Area in eastern Tennessee. Over thirty thousand people attended the two-day event, celebrating Cherokee traditions and culture. Coals from the sacred fire, carried west on the Trail of Tears, were brought back. These were added to coals carried from Qualla Boundary. A new sacred fire was lit with them in a special place on the hill. It connects the East with the West and the past with the present. It is hoped that it will burn for all time, as will the spirit of the Cherokees, a most adaptable people.

A CHEROKEE
CREATION STORY

The Cherokees told many stories about the creation of their land and the animals and people who lived in it. This is the tale of how the mountain home of the Cherokees was made.

Long, long ago, when This World was still young, there was a great flood that covered all the land. After some time, the waters went away, but there was no life on the land. When the creatures who lived in Galunlati (Upper World, or heaven) heard of this, they were pleased. For there were many of them in Galunlati, and it was crowded. They gathered in a great council to see what they should do. They decided to send someone down to This World to see if the story was true.

First the little insects tried to go. But they were too small and weak. They came back exhausted and said "We could not find the land. This idea will never work."

Then the small birds spoke up. "We can fly faster than the insects," they said. "We will find the land." But soon they too came back exhausted. "It is too far," they said. "We could not find the land."

Some bigger birds went next, but the same thing happened to them, for the land was very far away.

Finally the lowly buzzard spoke up. Now the buzzard did not often speak before the council of animals because he knew that the other creatures did not like him. They did not like the way he looked. And they didn't like what buzzards do.

But now the buzzard stepped before the council and this is what he said. "I have heard the story about the flood. And I know that some of you have tried to find the land but failed. But I think that I can find the land. The Great One who made me made my wings strong. I can fly far and fast. And I can glide for many miles so that my wings will not tire. I can go much farther than most of you. I can find the land."

Well, the other creatures did not want to believe that the buzzard could help them. But they did want to find the land, so they agreed that he should go.

Then the buzzard flew off in search of the land. He flew for many, many miles. At last he saw a land covered with mud from the floodwaters. He flew low to get a beak-full of mud to take back to the others.

He flew near the land, and as he did, his wings beat against the mud, carving great valleys in places and piling up mountains in others. And this is how the Great Smoky Mountains were made, the mountains that would become home to many creatures and to the Cherokee people.

And this is also why the Cherokees respect all living creatures, even the lowly buzzard.

IMPORTANT DATES

1000	Cherokee are well-established in Tennessee River/Great Smoky Mountain area, having come through the Appalachian Mountains on foot from Iroquois territory
1540	Hernando de Soto travels through Cherokee territory
1600s	First Spanish, then French and English explorers and traders begin to arrive in Cherokee territory
1730	A group of Cherokee leaders (including Attakullaculla) visit England
1754	Nanye hi rallies Cherokees in a battle against Creeks and becomes a Beloved Woman to her people
1756–1763	Cherokees fight with the British in the French and Indian War
1776	Cherokees again are allies of the British in the American Revolution
1780–1820	Numerous treaties are signed by the Cherokees giving up more and more land to the United States
1821	Sequoyah completes the Cherokee syllabary

1827	Cherokees draft a constitution modeled on that of the United States and declare themselves a nation
1828	The *Cherokee Phoenix* is first published; John Ross becomes Principal Chief; Andrew Jackson becomes President of the United States
1830	Indian Removal Act passed
1835	Major Ridge and a small group of Cherokees sign the Treaty of New Echota, selling all Cherokee land east of the Mississippi to the U.S. government
1838	Cherokees are forced to move to Indian Territory in a journey that becomes known as the Trail of Tears
1839	The Cherokee Nation establishes a new capital in what is now Oklahoma
1861	The Cherokee Nation is divided by the American Civil War and suffers greatly during and after the war
1868	Eastern Band officially recognized as a separate tribe from the Cherokee Nation in Oklahoma
1934	Great Smoky Mountain National Park is opened, providing a boost to the economy of the Eastern Band
1984	Eastern and Western Cherokee Councils meet at Red Clay, Tennessee
1985	Wilma Mankiller is elected Principal Chief of the Cherokee Nation
1987	Jonathan Taylor is elected Principal Chief of the Eastern Band
1988	One hundred and fifty years after the forced march of the Cherokee people, the Trail of Tears is named a National Landmark

GLOSSARY

Adawehis. A Cherokee holy man.

Ani Yun Wiya. The Cherokee name for themselves, meaning "the Principal People."

anthropologist. A person who studies the physical and cultural beginnings of groups of people.

asi. The small, round winter home of the Cherokees made from sticks lashed together and covered with a claylike mud called wattle and daub.

Beloved Woman. The name for a particularly respected female leader. A well-respected male leader might be called a Beloved Man.

booger. The name of a mask and special dance used by the Cherokees to make fun of their enemies and ward off evil.

Busk. The special ceremony held at the full-ripening of the corn crop. The celebration of the Busk marked the end of one year and the beginning of a new one.

epidemic. An outbreak of a serious disease in which many people are affected. After the arrival of the Europeans, many epidemics of cholera, smallpox, and other deadly diseases wiped out whole towns and most members of some tribes.

gadugi. A group of Cherokee workers who share their resources and look after one another.

Galunlati. The Cherokee word for Upper World, or heaven.

Ghigau. The Cherokee word for Beloved Woman.

Iroquoian. The group of languages from which the Cherokee language comes.

mixed-blood. A person whose ancestors come from different racial groups. Many of the descendants of the Cherokee people today are of mixed blood. That is, they have ancestors of both Indian and non-Indian races.

Muskogean. The group of languages that most of the Cherokees' neighbors spoke.

syllabary. The kind of alphabet Sequoyah developed for the Cherokee language. In a syllabary, each sound or syllable in the spoken language is given a symbol.

Uktena. An evil creature of Cherokee legend.

ulunsuti. A crystal scale from the Uktena, said to bring good luck to anyone who had one.

BIBLIOGRAPHY

*Books for children

Brown, Virginia Pounds, and Laurella Owens. *The World of the Southern Indians.* Leeds, Ala.: Beechwood Books, 1983.

Burt, Jesse, and Robert B. Ferguson. *Indians of the Southeast: Then and Now.* Nashville, Tenn.: Abingdon Press, 1973.

*Carpenter, Allen. *Oklahoma.* Chicago: Childrens Press, 1979. Also by the same author in the New Enchantment of America series, *Georgia* (1979), *Tennessee* (1978), and *North Carolina* (1979).

Dykeman, Wilma, and Jim Stokely. *Highland Homeland: The People of the Great Smokies.* Washington, D.C.: National Park Services, 1978.

Finger, John R. *Cherokee Americans, The Eastern Band of the Cherokees in the Twentieth Century.* Lincoln: University of Nebraska Press, 1991.

Galloway, Mary Regina Ulmer, editor. *Aunt Mary, Tell Me a Story: A Collection of Cherokee Legends and Tales as told by Mary Ulmer Chiltoskey.* Cherokee, N.C.: Cherokee Communications, 1990.

*Glassman, Bruce. *Wilma Mankiller: Chief of the Cherokee Nation.* Milwaukee: Raintree Publishers, 1991.

*Hofsinde, Robert (Gray-Wolf). *Indian Arts.* New York: William Morrow and Co., 1971.

Josephy, Alvin M. Jr., editor. *The American Heritage Book of Indians.* Charlotte, N.C.: Heritage Publishing Co., 1961.

Mason, Bernard S. *The Book of Indian Arts and Crafts.* New York: The Ronald Press Co., 1946.

Maxwell, James A., editor. *America's Fascinating Indian Heritage.* New York: The Reader's Digest Assoc. Inc., 1978.

*McCall, Barbara A. *The Cherokee.* Vero Beach, Fla.: Rourke Publications, 1989.

*Ortiz, Simon. *The People Shall Continue.* Chicago: Childrens Press, 1988.

*Patterson, Lillie. *Sequoyah, The Cherokee Who Captured Words.* Champaign, Ill.: Garrard Publishing Co., 1975.

*Perdue, Theda. *The Cherokee.* New York: Chelsea House Publishers, 1989.

*Petersen, David. *Sequoyah, Father of the Cherokee Alphabet.* Chicago: Childrens Press, 1991.

Slapin, Beverly, and Doris Seale. *Through Indian Eyes: The Native Experience in Books for Children.* Philadelphia: New Society Publishers, 1992.

*Tamarin, Alfred. *We Have Not Vanished: Eastern Indians of the United States.* Chicago: Follett Press, 1974.

Woodward, Grace Steele. *The Cherokee.* Norman: University of Oklahoma Press, 1963.

INDEX

Page numbers in *italics* refer to illustrations.